Christian Unity 101
A Guide to Finding the One Holy Universal Christian Church Within Its Many Branches

Dr. Byron Perrine

With illustrations from the writings of

Rev. William Harness and

Baptist Wriothesley Noel

This book is Volume 3 of Our Christian Heritage Foundation's Historical Reprints Series.

Also available from Our Christian Heritage Foundation:

The Religion that Shaped America, Dr. Byron Perrine, Editor.

Emerson's Evangelical Primer, by Joseph Emerson, Vol. 1 of Our Christian Heritage Foundation's Historical Reprints Series.

Memoir of Catharine Brown—A Christian Indian of the Cherokee Nation, by Rufus Anderson, Vol. 2 of Our Christian Heritage Foundation's Historical Reprints Series.

Copyright © 2013 Our Christian Heritage Foundation

All rights reserved.

ISBN: 10: 0615745962
ISBN-13: 978-0615745961

CONTENTS

1 Introductory Remarks by the Rev. Dr. Byron Perrine, Founder of Our Christian Heritage Foundation — 1

2 The "Visible" Church and the "Invisible" Church by Dr. Byron Perrine — 5

3 Christian Unity—A Practicable Christian Duty by the Rev. W. Harness (One Example of an Argument in support of one's own particular "Visible" Church without regard for or sensitivity to the "Invisible" Church—This Approach Not Recommended!) — 9

4 The Unity of the Church by Baptist Wriothesley Noel (One Example of an Argument in support of the "Invisible" Church—This Approach Highly Recommended!) — 45

5 A Call to Live With Integrity Within the Discipline of One's particular Manifestation of the Visible Church while at the same time Recognizing, Affirming and Serving the One Holy Universal Christian Church — 66

ACKNOWLEDGEMENTS

Reprinted as part of this work are the following historical works:

Noel, Baptist Wriothesley. The Unity of the Church, Another Tract for the Times, Addressed Especially to Members of the Establishment. London: James Nisbet and Co., 1838.

Harness, Rev. W. Christian Unity—A Practicable Christian Duty: The Substance of Two Sermons Preached at All Saints' Church, Knightsbridge. Westminster: Vacher & Sons, 1852.
(We have somewhat abridged this tract for use in our present publication.)

CHAPTER 1.
INTRODUCTORY REMARKS
by the Rev. Dr. Byron Perrine, Founder
Our Christian Heritage Foundation

The Problem

Of all the objections and proofs raised against the Christian Church probably the most damaging is the evidence of disunity and division. Given that there are so many different "churches" claiming to represent the "true way" in their theology, liturgical practice, church polity and governance, disparaging those who differ in theology, liturgical practice and church polity and governance, and given the human frailty and sinfulness of the members of all of these various "churches", how can any of them be claim superiority, how can others accept their claim to superiority, and how can seemingly irreconcilable differences be bridged to achieve Christian unity between these various, and often antithetical groups be achieved?

Definitions

The theology, liturgical practice, church polity and governance of the various Christian groups constitute outward manifestations of the church. These manifestations are the "visible church". Underlying them all is one holy universal Christian church which constitutes the "invisible church". All "visible churches" are to some extent manifestations, though imperfectly, of the "invisible church". All true Christians are members of the invisible church regardless of the visible manifestation of the church with which they may or may not be affiliated. Within every visible church may be found members of the invisible church, the one holy universal Christian church.

The Premise

Certain visible churches may claim that adherence to a uniform standard of theology, liturgical practice, church polity and governance is necessary for one to be a member of the one holy universal Christian church. This is, however, incorrect. It is more correct to state simply that there it is necessary to adhere to a standard of theology, liturgical practice, polity and governance in order to be a part of a given visible branch of the church and that there may be advantages therein, but failure to do so in no way precludes a person from being a part of the invisible church. Uniformity of theology, liturgical practice, church polity and governance is therefore unnecessary. It is also impossible to achieve. Moreover, it is most probably not even desirable. Unity of Spirit is, however, necessary, possible, and desirable. This unity is to be achieved by learning to recognize the signs of the invisible church in others who differ from us in theology, liturgical practice, church polity and governance.

The Method

This book will begin by setting forth in greater detail the editor's observations which hopefully will open the heart and mind of the reader to the recognition of the marks of the invisible church in Christians found among the various visible churches. In addition, two historical essays will be offered as illustrative of opposite approaches to dealing with the differences that separate Christians—the essay by Harness is provided as illustrative example of an approach aimed at achieving Christian unity by silencing dissent; in contrast, the essay by Noel is provided as an illustrative example of an approach that sees unity of spirit possible in the midst of diversity, and which provides suitable guidelines for achieving that unity. It is hoped that the contrast provided by Harness's essay will serve to accentuate the superior quality of Noel's approach.

No doubt countless other essays might be found illustrative of the principles presented in Noel's essay. The goal of the book, however, rather than providing many written examples, is to stimulate the reader to develop an appreciation for *living* examples, persons found within one's own "visible" church who are also a part of the "invisible" church, the one holy universal Christian church. This is the foundational principle upon which true Christian unity is to be built, and, it is the first and essential lesson of Christian Unity 101.

CHAPTER 2.
THE "VISIBLE" CHURCH
AND THE "INVISIBLE" CHURCH
by Dr. Byron Perrine

"Visible Churches", while authoritative to those who are joined within that body, are nonetheless metaphors, incomplete visible representations of that more perfect thing to which they point. Just as the Holy Spirit is invisible except for its effect, so too there has from the beginning been a church that is invisible. Actually, it is a church within the churches. It is made up of many who in obedience to the Holy Spirit have sought and are seeking the homeland of the heart (Hebrews 11:13-16). Such have been called not from only one creed or denomination, rather out of the many.

Both the visible and invisible churches have a place and purpose in the life of the believer. The one preserves historical integrity, the other stretches forth in mending and in new growth.

From the beginning, the Holy Spirit has been working as leaven among us (Luke 13:20-21). This fermentation has caused tension (Matthew 10:34-39) between the visible church and those responding to the

Holy Spirit who strives to bring to fruition the new creation of our Lord. Visible churches, by their very nature, tend toward pattern maintenance seeking to preserve through institutions from one generation to the next the great truths they have found to be meaningful to them, this in contrast to other additional work of the Holy Spirit which "blows where it wishes" (John 3:8).

The many churches and the whole world itself have been in travail (Romans 8:22-28). As Augustine wrote in his Exposition on Psalm 53, "who there is in this world that travaileth and is in pain, the faithful acknowledge, because thereof they are. Christ here travaileth, Christ here is in pain: the Head is above, the members below. For one not travailing nor in pain would not say, 'Saul, Saul, why persecutes thou me?' Him, with whom when persecuting He was travailing, being converted, (Acts 9:4) He made to travail. For he also was himself afterwards enlightened, and grafted on those members which he used to persecute; being pregnant with the same love, he said, 'My little children, of whom again I travail, until Christ be formed in you' (Galatians 4:19). For the members of Christ, for His Body which is the Church (Colossians 1:24), for the same One Man, that is, for that very unity, whereof the Head is above, this Psalm is sung…. Who are they, then, amid whom we travail and groan, if in the Body of Christ we are, if under Him, the Head, we live, if amongst His members we are counted? Who they are, hear ye." But in the fullness of time that which is hidden is now being revealed. The journey is not yet complete but is nearing completion (I Corinthians 13:12).

In addition to the visible churches and the invisible church, there is a third church. This is the church of the anti-Christ, who having the form of Christianity lack its substance (Matthew 7:21-23). Those who join themselves voluntarily with this body condemn themselves by having shut their heart to the Holy Spirit. The judgment they bring upon themselves is that when unresponsive to the Holy Spirit there can be no change, no new life, no growth into the more perfect likeness of Christ, no redemption, no salvation. Being a part of this body cannot be forgiven (Matthew 12:31-32) for that reason—those who shut their heart to the Holy Spirit bring death through stagnation upon themselves. We are intended to be reborn into the likeness of Christ which is impossible when the Holy Spirit is shut out.

In the church of the anti-Christ, just about anything goes. There are no eternal truths, no natural law, the teachings of the general and special revelations are ignored or paid "lip service" only, the guidance of the Holy Spirit is not sought, there are no crucial teachings to be contemplated and understood with the help of the Holy Spirit. The essentials of true Christianity are replaced with mindless distortions. Integrity is compromised in the name of pluralism. The innocent are seduced into apostasy by the misuse of platitudes such as "tolerance for diversity" and "freedom of conscience" which in the hands of the unscrupulous become seductive euphemisms for the debunking of all natural law and disregard for revealed religion.

Beware! If an epistemology of the Holy Spirit is impossible within the church, that church is not truly Christian. Because they are not seeking, they will not find. And because they have closed the door to the Holy Spirit they cannot be found.

Moreover, such persons seek to shut the kingdom of

heaven against others… they seek to prevent those who are entering to go in, they seek to silence the testimony of the Holy Spirit, they will travel across sea and land to make a single proselyte, and when a proselyte is found take delight in making that person twice as much a child of hell as themselves. Beware of these ravenous wolves who present themselves to you in sheep's clothing (Matthew 7:13-20).

Editor's Note Regarding Chapter 3

The following essay by William Harness illustrates one way of dealing with the problem of Christian disunity. His suggestion, dismiss differences of opinion regarding religious doctrines and practices as being presumptuous and speculative and therefore not to be dignified by being taken seriously. I suppose that if one is so inclined, dictating "uniformity" as a substitute for "unity" might achieve some purpose. I very much doubt, however, that such an approach accomplishes anything more than shutting the door to the leading of the Holy Spirit, to say nothing of reinforcing obnoxious chauvinistic behavior, and theological laziness. But then, this is "Church Unity 101". Try it on and see if it works for you.

CHAPTER 3.

CHRISTIAN UNITY—A PRACTICABLE CHRISTIAN DUTY
(Somewhat abridged)
by the Rev. W. Harness
(One Example of an Argument in support of one's particular "Visible" Church without regard for or sensitivity to the "Invisible" Church—This Approach Not Recommended!)

"Be ye all of one mind."—1 Peter 3:8

"Few men," says Bishop Taylor, "consider, that so long as men have such variety of principles, such several constitutions, educations, tempers and distempers; hopes, interests and weaknesses, degrees of light and degrees of understanding, it is *impossible* all should be of one mind; and what is impossible to be done, is not necessary it should be done." This opinion is wonderfully popular. It recommends itself to our adoption by its tone of liberality; it affords excuse for a great many schismatical differences in others; it grants immunity to a multitude of wild religious conjectures of our own; but the license which it offers is more accordant with the spirit of the world than the spirit of Christianity, and is hardly compatible with the express letter of the sacred Scriptures. St. Peter, in my text, charges us "to be all of one mind"; St. Paul exhorts us "all to speak the same thing," and "to allow of no divisions"; and our Lord, on the eve of leaving his disciples, made it the subject of his affecting prayer, that they "all might be one, even as he and his Father are one."

Now these passages would lead us to infer, that unanimity of doctrine among Christians cannot be, as Bishop Taylor has asserted, a blessing absolutely placed above our reach. We cannot piously believe that St. Peter and St. Paul would so earnestly have impressed upon us, as members of Christ's Church, the duty of being like-minded, or that our Savior would have entreated his heavenly Father to assist us with his grace in fulfilling that duty, if, notwithstanding our own endeavors and God's help, "it was a thing impossible to be done, and therefore not necessary to be done."

But if to be of *one mind* is a practicable Christian duty, it is manifest that we, who profess to be members of Christ's Church, and who nevertheless are all of *different minds,* must be guilty of a very serious violation of our Christian duty. But we do not, in this respect, apprehend the weight of our responsibility. Disagreement in religion is so common, that we have learnt to look upon it as a very venial offence. Agreement in religion is thought to be so difficult, that we hold ourselves absolved from making any efforts to attain it. But, unhappily, our estimate of the offence will not mitigate its guilt. Our unchristian dissensions constitute a very grave transgression. They are not only directly opposed to the will of God, but they operate most perniciously to the interests of the Gospel; and as we would fulfill his will and advance his glory, it is incumbent on us to consider in this matter what our conduct has been, to repent of what we have done amiss, and to repair it as far as possible, by making every effort in our power for the restoration of Christian peace. The task may be difficult; but of its difficulty we can know nothing, for we have never made any attempt to master it. On the contrary, instead of trying to reconcile, we are always trying to aggravate our differences; and I do not believe that unanimity would be found impossible or even difficult, if, reforming our present habit of fomenting mutual animosity, and acting under a proper sense of our religious duty in this respect, we would only give a fair consideration to the immense importance of the points on which we are agreed, and the doubtful, speculative nature of the points on which we differ.

    Consider, in the first place, the extent and the importance of the points on which we are agreed. Premising that my observations are exclusively addressed to members of the Church of England, it may, I apprehend, be taken for granted, that we are "all of one mind" so far as to yield a full and cordial assent to the doctrines which are comprised in the Apostles' Creed. I assume that such an agreement exists among us; as I have never heard any man, professing to be a member of the English Church, who has questioned any part of that brief, simple, and comprehensive summary of the Christian faith. It is called the Apostles' Creed because the Church has always held it in reverence as the symbol, which, in the main, was composed in apostolic times and by apostolic men, if not actually agreed upon by the Apostles themselves. It is believed by many to be identical with that "form of sound words" in which St. Timothy was instructed by St. Paul, and which he was charged to "hold fast". The opinion of the Christian world respecting the high authority of this creed is confirmed by the fact, that all the early Churches of Christendom retained this form of "sound words" as a sacred deposit which each had received at its first formation, and which was maintained by each without any variation of doctrine, and with only such inconsiderable differences of expression as would inevitably arise from its transmission through different languages. At your baptism, this creed enunciated the faith of which profession was made in your name. In your childhood, this creed comprised the scheme of religion which you learnt with your Catechism. At your confirmation, this was the creed which, as a candidate for that holy rite, you were expected to know and to accept. In attending the Lord's Table as a communicant, your Church requires nothing more of you, her lay members, with regard to your belief, than the profession of the sacred truths which that creed declares. And, if we all receive and heartily assent to this creed of the Apostles, as I apprehend is the case, we all receive and heartily assent to the great fundamental and essential articles of a saving faith. To what an immense extent, then, are we already "of one mind"!

Why, when Irenaeus asserted, at the end of the second century, that "the Churches disseminated over the world, having received the preaching of the faith, preserved it diligently, as the inhabitants of one house; believed it alike as having the same soul and heart, and delivered it alike as having the same mouth": —when he declared that the Churches of Germany "neither believed nor taught otherwise than those which were in Spain, in France, in the East, in Egypt, or in the middle of the world; but, as one and the same sun shone through the whole earth, so did the light of one and the same truth disperse itself": —when this venerable father thus boasted of the unanimity of Christian people, what constituted the bond of faith, by which they were united? My friends, that catholic bond of union was found in the catholic profession of the Apostles' Creed. This, in his days, was the only religious symbol known among Christians. Till Arius, by his heretical doctrines respecting the nature of our Lord, drew forth those explanatory additions which were inserted at the Councils of Constantinople and Nicaea in the early part of the fourth century, no other formulary of doctrine existed in the Church; and, if we are *"of one mind"* with regard to the articles of faith asserted in that creed, we are *"of one mind"* as far as the Apostles and their immediate disciples held unanimity to be essential; and *"we are of one mind"* as truly as the members of the primitive Church were of *"one mind."*

I have said, that this creed was the only abstract of their religious tenets generally received among Christians till the beginning of the fourth century. The Nicene

Creed was then drawn up. In it the terms of the Apostles' Creed were amplified on the authority of the Scriptures, and almost in the words of Scripture. This creed, which is read every Sunday in the Communion Service, conveys the explanatory comment of the Church on the articles of the primitive faith; it was designed to preclude all future controversy among Christians respecting those vital points of religion which Arius and his sect had brought into dispute. It was deliberated on and approved by the Council of Nicaea; it was confirmed in subsequent Councils; it was declared to be final at the Council of Ephesus; it has, with the exception of a single word… been held in reverence ever since, during a period of 1500 years, by both the Eastern and Western Churches;* and is, in all probability, there is not a single member of our Church who will feel disposed to question the strictly scriptural view of Gospel truth which it presents, I again call on you to observe the number and the importance of the points on which we are already *"of one mind."*

There is another creed, the Athanasian. This summary of doctrine is an enlargement of the Nicene Creed, as the Nicene is an enlargement of the Apostles' Creed. Every addition that has been made in it refers to some heretical opinion, against which the rulers of the Church desired to guard the minds of their flock. The origin of this creed is uncertain; and it has never been sanctioned by any General Council; but the propositions it declares will, I think be admitted by all who entertain a pious reverence for the New Testament, because they are

---

*The only difference between the Western and Eastern Churches, with regard to this creed, is found in the clause relating to the procession of the Holy Ghost….

apostles, and are therefore established on the certainty of fair deductions from the words of Jesus Christ and his Scripture. In fact, the Athanasian Creed contains the same doctrines as the Apostles' and Nicene Creeds; but expresses them with a strict and exact precision of language, for the sake of obviating every conceivable variety of misapprehension respecting them. Of these three symbols, it has been said, that the faith of the Church is *declared* in the first, *explained* in the second, and *defended* in the third. It is, I am aware, a question with many, whether a composition such as the Athanasian Creed, of which the language is rather that of the theological school than of the temple of Christian worship—which rather resembles in its construction an ingenious exposition of heretical errors than a simple declaration of Evangelical truths—is fitted for congregational use. This is a question well worthy of consideration; but I apprehend it is not one of doctrine, but of expediency. It is simply confined to the terms in which the doctrines are conveyed, and does not touch the subject matter of the creed.

Now if we are all of one mind with regard to the substance of these venerable creeds, I cannot help believing that all pious, reasonable, and not presumptuous members of our Church—who look upon religion in its proper light, not as a matter of curious speculation, but as an exalted principle of action—are agreed on every point with regard to which agreement is necessary or can probably be obtained, without further information from above. The Gospel is designed to restore the union between man and God; to raise our affections from temporal to eternal blessings; to place our souls in intimate relation with the spiritual world; and to afford us such guidance and assistance as we may require in the course of our Christian progress. The doctrines by which the creature is thus connected with his Creator, earth with heaven, time with eternity, are set before us at large in the sacred Scriptures, and from them, for our more distinct and ready apprehension, they have been collected in the creeds; and it is quite inconceivable, how any man who is in accord with his brother Christian on matters so important, should be able to discover any sufficient grounds for the disturbance of charity on matters so insignificant as those which become the ordinary occasions of difference: nor, if his charity were such as a Christian ought to possess, do I believe that he could. All the members of our Church who "hold fast these forms of sound words," are bound together in the bonds of a holy brotherhood, as worshippers of the same God, as redeemed by the same Savior, and as sanctified by the same Spirit; and, if Christian in disposition as in name, in charity as by profession, they would no more quarrel among themselves, because, in addressing the same Almighty Being, the one turned to the east, and the other to the west; because, in uttering the same prayers and thanksgivings, they were said by the one, and chanted by the other; or because, in delivering the same doctrines, the one was dressed in black, and the other in white—than they could separate themselves from their dearest relative on account of the color of his hair, or the tone of his voice, or the tint of his complexion. No: only give their due weight and consideration to the eternal truths of religion on which we are agreed, and even the weakness and folly of human nature itself must be brought to a conviction that the mere externals of religion are, when compared with them, far too immaterial to differ about.

But though we all hold the doctrines delivered by these creeds in their integrity, and without addition or diminution, may not questions arise which are very far from being so immaterial as I have stated, and which would afford very justifiable grounds of difference? I answer, No; and without any hesitation. I differ from the Romanists; and why? Because they have added no less than twelve articles to the creed which, from the time of the Apostles to the Council of Trent, a space of no less than 1500 years, was the faith of the Church. I also differ from the Dissenters; and why? Because, with the exception of the first article of the creed, which declares the existence of "God, the Father Almighty," there is no article which is not impugned by some; while the belief in "on holy, catholic, and apostolic Church," is repudiated by all. But I cannot entertain any religious difference with those of my brother Christians and fellow-churchmen who maintain the faith of the creeds as we have received them at the hands of the saints and martyrs of early times; because the questions agitated, when not, as I have already said, of slight and immaterial consequence, are questions raised so immeasurably above the range of my knowledge, that I hold it presumptuous to discuss, and impossible to determine them.

For where does this debatable land of Christianity begin? Among us Churchmen it begins precisely at the point where the creeds end. We cannot advance a step beyond the few simple elements of revealed truth contained in these primitive formularies of faith, without involving ourselves in some obscure theme of religious speculation, on which the Bible has intimated little, but of which, though that little is as much, in all probability, as we need know or can possibly understand, we are anxious to know more. The occasions of dispute arise when we venture to treat with too inquisitive a spirit the union and distinction of the Trinity; the mystery of original sin, the extent and nature of its entailed corruption; the inscrutable operations of the Holy Ghost; or the compatibility of the foreknowledge of God and the fixed counsels of his providence, with the freedom of human will and the responsibility of human conduct. Such are the questions which afford the dark and unfathomable source of all our numberless divisions. We only cease to be of one mind; when we allow our minds to be occupied with subjects on which the disclosures of Scripture are not ample enough to satisfy our curiosity, and of which the discussion must necessarily be interminable, because we are neither acquainted with all the circumstances which constitute the facts of the case; nor are we capable of ascertaining them; nor, if ascertained, would the obtuse and limited capacities of our reason be competent to the apprehension of them.

I would refer, for instance, to the nature of the Deity. How is it possible that our understandings, bounded as their faculties are, and receiving all their ideas from only five apertures of sense, and within a very confined range of experience, should arrive at any conception of that invisible Power who is the Author of everything we see around us? His works assure us that he is powerful, and wise, and good; but of the Divine essence, or nature, we know no more than he has vouchsafed to reveal in the Scriptures; and from them we learn no more concerning the triune mystery of his being—of the Father, whom we have offended; of the Son, who has effected our reconciliation; and of the Holy Ghost, by whom we are sanctified—than is necessary to be told us for the welfare of our souls. Such disclosures, when made, are not made for the purpose of satisfying our theological curiosity, but with a view to our religious improvement. They are not addressed to the mind, but the heart. The human intellect cannot deal with them; it has no faculty to embrace such spiritual matters, and it has no words to represent them. The sacred writers, in speaking of the Godhead—the Father, the Son, and the Holy Spirit—are compelled, for the sake of bringing their high argument at all within our reach, to express themselves in terms which are merely figurative; which are adopted from relations existing among ourselves; which are liable to be mistaken if too literally interpreted; and which, even when rightly understood, can only impart a very dim and distant idea of spiritual truth. Of God's attributes, of his power, goodness, mercy, and justice—with which we are all immediately concerned—we read much in the Bible; but of the nature of the Divine Being to whom those attributes appertain, we only meet with a few and scattered intimations. It is conceived that there is something inconsistent in these intimations. Ingenious men, "stretching themselves beyond their measure," have devised various schemes by which these apparently inconsistent intimations may be reconciled; and most mischievous have been the consequences. By their presumptuous attempts to explore the inscrutable and to define the ineffable, they have become the originators of schisms in the Church; whereas, on matters which are so totally beyond the scan of human reason, there is only one safe course to follow—to confine our thoughts to the notices of revelation, and our language to the very expressions of the sacred Scriptures. In treating of arguments so exalted, the use of any terms of our own invention is dangerous. We can no more set forth the mysteries of the Divine essence in human words than we can represent the substance of the Deity by human portraiture. On such subjects the Christian can have but one duty, and that is to receive with reverence the instructions of God's Word, and to adore with a silent consciousness of his own intellectual weakness. If we look downward to the inferior creatures, we find ourselves incapable of explaining the instinct of the ant or of the bee; if, then, we venture to speculate on the nature of any higher order of existence—I speak not of the Divine, but even of the angelic, nature, —how can we as reasonable beings, expect to derive any other result from our presumptuous speculations than bewilderment and defeat?

Again, with regard to the question which now, in a more especial manner, agitates the Church—I mean baptismal regeneration—what say the Scriptures? Our Savior sent forth his Apostles "to make disciples among all nations," and promised that "whosoever believed and was baptized should be saved." St. Paul, in his Epistle to Titus, calls the sacrament of baptism "the washing of regeneration." In the First Epistle to the Corinthians, he assures the members of that Church that "by one Spirit they are all baptized into one body." St. Peter, on the day of Pentecost, exhorted the Jews "to repent and be baptized in the name of Jesus Christ, for "to repent and be baptized in the name of Jesus Christ, for the remission of sins." And with a few and recent exceptions—*few* as compared with the myriads of Christians, and *recent* as compared with the 1800 years that the Christian religion has existed—the whole Church has concluded, according to the natural sense of these and other similar expressions of our Lord and his Apostles, that the believing and repentant convert, when admitted by baptism into the pale of the Church of Christ, becomes cleansed of the guilt of his past sins, and is brought into communion with the Spirit of Christ. This doctrine is clear and intelligible…. On what grounds, then, is the doctrine of baptismal regeneration impugned? Do any Churchmen doubt, in defiance of all scriptural authority, whether there is as our creed declares, "one baptism for the remission of sins"? (None) but inquisitive men, "stretching themselves beyond their measure"…. My brethren, God, in the Bible, speaks simply to his creatures. He does not address them with the subtleties of a casuist, or the refinements of a theologian. He delivers his laws in a few, plain, and intelligible words….

But so thoroughly are all spiritual things, if we venture to extend our thoughts ever so little beyond what is written, incomprehensible to the human intellect, that those scholastic theologians who are considered, according to our narrow views, to maintain the most opposite opinions, may not improbably be both partially right, and only altogether wrong in their contests with each other. Such is, I conceive, the case with regard to predestination. The Calvinist is right in asserting the immutability of God's decrees; the Arminian is right in insisting on the necessity of man's co-operation. The righteous are predestined to attain a state of eternal happiness; and yet that state depends on their own exertions. The proposition appears to be self-contradictory; but, if we believe the Bible, we must admit it to be true. Text after text might be cited in confirmation of both clauses of the proposition....

Who shall comprehend these things? They are too great and excellent for us. Men of ingenious minds, not content to be ignorant where knowledge is impossible, and "stretching themselves beyond their measure," try to account for the difficulties that they involve; and each, differing from the other, assists in giving rise to some new schism among our Lord's disciples. But the Christian who would walk humbly with his God has no concern in such vain devices. His duty is practical, not speculative; and it engages him to trust that God, by whose mercy he is placed in the ark of Christ's Church, has decreed his salvation; and to abide in the vessel, working out his salvation with fear and trembling, in the humble hope of finding the Divine decree in his favor fulfilled at the last day.

In all those subjects, which are in dispute among us Churchmen, the disputants are indulging in presumptuous speculation, and "stretching themselves beyond their measure." They are dealing with matters too high for the human reason. All such subtleties are left untouched in those brief abstracts of Christian doctrine which were considered sufficient for the early Church; within the limits of which the secure tract of ascertainable truth is comprised; and beyond which we no sooner venture to range than we enter the precincts of metaphysical theology—a lofty, barren, and misty region of thought, on which the majority of those who attempt it only rise so far as to become involved in the clouds, and to see then less the higher they ascend; while few, if any, ever reach a sufficient elevation to expatiate in the enjoyment of a more tine, and pure, and ethereal religious light.

Now, with regard to all such questions as appear to

originate in the obscure speculations of metaphysical theology, what is the course which, as Christians, you should adopt? It is your duty, remember, to obey as far as possible the exhortation of the Apostle, and endeavor to be "all of one mind." It is your duty to advance, by every means in your power, the accomplishment of our Savior's prayer for the unanimity of his disciples; and my first advice would be, to abstain from the consideration of such questions altogether. They can neither help you in discharging your Christian duties, nor in attaining the Christian character; they cannot, therefore, have any reference to the all-important work of your salvation. But if, in an age so controversial as the present, such a passive position be found untenable, shall I, a minister of the English Church, be considered as exacting too much of you, who profess to be members of that Church, if, for the sake of promoting so invaluable an object as the peace of our Church, I implore you, as fair and honest men, to take the trouble of making yourselves thoroughly acquainted with the state of the argument on both sides, before you venture to mingle in the discussion of those subjects on which theological differences have arisen?

There is only one science in which the uninformed and the misinformed claim equal privilege with the well informed to argue and decide upon disputed questions, and that science is theology: in this, the most difficult of all, such interference is universal. The practice is not confined to society, it extends to literature; it not only prevails in the conversation of the religious world, but it may be observed in the publications of the different religious parties. We find the writers on either side attributing opinions to each other which were never entertained; stating their adversaries' views in terms which those adversaries indignantly repudiate; and assuming that they have exposed the unsoundness of doctrines to which they object, by the refutation of arguments which its adherents had never used in its support. Most pernicious are the effects of this license of ignorance. Its results are mutual misapprehension, a widening of the vast gulf by which the opponents are severed, and a continual increase of party bitterness and irritation. We should have made a most blessed advance towards the restoration of the peace of the Church, if none would engage in any of its controversies except those by whom the matter under discussion is, in all its depth and height and bearing, perfectly understood; and if every other, keeping the bond of Christian charity unimpaired, would observe a strict neutrality, and, instead of aggravating the animosity of the debate by the encouragement of his mischievous partisanship, would endeavor, with the gentle counsels of a brother and a Christian, to allay the irritate feelings of the disputants.

Giving their due weight to all those important articles of faith on which we are agreed, and which afford the most persuasive inducements to charity; and keeping an impartial silence with regard to all those disputed questions on which we are either altogether ignorant, or only superficially informed, there is another measure which is completely in your power, and which you are bound to adopt for the sake of promoting the tranquility of the Church—I mean the extending towards those whose sentiments may not exactly correspond with your own, the most ample indulgence which is compatible with the integrity of Christian truth and the purity of Christian morals.

Now here I would observe, that though this charitable

toleration is a general duty imperative on all Christians towards all mankind, it is, for reasons which I shall endeavor to make evident, more especially the duty of the members of the English Church towards each other. It is demanded of us by the very constitution of our Church....

Our Church became what it is in the very brightest era of the English intellect. At a time when strong, energetic, manly good sense was the characteristic of the English people; when the sound mind delighted to entertain the thought of vast and arduous enterprises, and the sound body felt itself capable of achieving them; when Bacon, by the vigor of his understanding, set Philosophy free from the region of misty speculations within which she had been for centuries confined, and brought her into contact with realities; when Shakespeare invested the maxims of a moral wisdom which can never perish in the beauties of a poetry which can never be surpassed; when our island was fruitful of such men, and her people were capable of appreciating their worth, our national Church received her present form and rule of government—her Liturgy, her Offices, her Homilies, and her Articles; and every document which interprets her mind bears the stamp of the masculine intellect of the period during which her restoration was gradually perfected. The peculiar characteristic of the Church of England is derived from that *sound common sense* which was the dominant quality of the age of her spiritual revival, and by which all her great authorities were distinguished.

This sound common sense was evinced in everything that our Reformers did, and it imparted consistency to measures which were carried on by different agents, under different reigns, and without any preconcerted design; it was evinced in the moderation which led them not to destroy the existing constitution of the Church, but to seek out, by the light of Scripture and the remains of the early Fathers, what had been the form of religion bequeathed to the world by the Apostles, and to restore to the Church of England that form of pure apostolic religion; it was evinced in the measures they adopted for suppressing by degrees, and without violently offending the prejudices of the people, every superstitious observance or erroneous doctrine; it was evinced in the reverence with which they retained every particular relating to ecclesiastical government of discipline, of which the existence from the beginning could be proved; and it was further evinced in that perfect fairness, in that freedom from party bias, and in that absence of all tendency to systematize, which the most cursory observer must discern in our Articles and our Liturgy. The Church of England presents such a view of the Gospel revelation as any company of learned, sensible, and pious men would take who looked to the holy Scriptures for the ground of their opinions, and who, whenever a matter of doubt arose, acted as any such a body of men would act, and referred the solution of the doubt to the authority of primitive antiquity. The religion which they have delivered to us is neither Papistical, nor Lutheran, nor Calvinistic, nor Arminian, nor Socinian; it is purely Scriptural, Christian, and Catholic.

But if this sound common sense of our Reformers be so manifest in everything of human appointment as to constitute one of the most striking characteristics of our Church, we must admit that this, its distinguishing excellent, is not without its accompanying evil. Our national form of Christianity seems to be more especially framed for one description of our Lord's disciples. None appear to be contemplated as members of her communion except those who have been born of Christian parents, and education on Christian principles; who gratefully accept the Gospel as an hereditary possession, with a pure conscience and an entire conviction of its truth; who reverence it as the divinely appointed rule by which the actions, affections, and appetites of their human nature must be governed; who look to its counsels for direction in the emergencies, and for support under the sorrows, of this life; who are diligently discharging the duties of that station in which it has pleased God to place them; and who have no more grave offences to reproach themselves with than such lapses of inadvertency or surprise as the weakness of human nature is never free from, and as their Heavenly Father will not be extreme in imputing to their charge. For this class of our Lord's disciples—the highest, the best, and also the most rate—our Church has provided. She has fully considered their spiritual needs; but she has been too little careful of all others. She offers a home for the healthy, for the disciples of regular affections and sound intellect; but where is her asylum for the infirm, for the disciple of stricken conscience, or of unduly balanced understanding?

For the perpetrator of some egregious act of wickedness, who, suddenly awakened to the horror of its guilt, is haunted day and night by the phantom of his secret sin, and who would fain express the sense of his iniquity and the sincerity of his contrition in the exercises of a penitential religion; for the enthusiast, of whose mind the stupendous truths of the Gospel have taken such an active possession as renders him careless of the advantages of the present time, and incapable of applying himself heartily to any occupation unless it have an immediate bearing on the blessings of eternity; for the disappointed, who have tried the world and experienced its vanity, who have relied on promises and proved their falsehood, who have expected to rise by favor and found themselves ruined by caprice, and who at length would place all their hopes in attaining the glories of Heaven, and dedicate themselves to the service of their God; for the imaginative, who almost live in an ideal world, and who pine after devotional services, rich in the embellishments of art, by which their aspirations may be assisted in soaring above the realities of this earth and ascending nearer, as they conceive, to an apprehension of the glories of Heaven; for the irresolute and the weak-minded, who are readily withdrawn from all thought of religion, unless religion be adopted as the business of their life; for the solitary mourner, whom the death of relatives and friends has bereaved of every interest on this side of the grave, but to whom each loss as it occurred imparted an interest deeper and more deep in the regions which lie beyond it; for these, and a multitude such as these, whose moral state demands our Christian care and tenderness, the Church of England has virtually made no provision. It does not seem to have contemplated their existence; it has assigned them no appropriate place; it is essentially the religion of common sense; it addresses itself to men and women of common sense; it is admirably adapted to the regular routine, and the daily recurring exigencies, of common life; but it never seems to have taken those cases into consideration which, though exceptional and extraordinary, are of frequent occurrence. It has had regard for one phase of the religious character, and has overlooked the requirements of every other.

Now, while I make this statement, I am nevertheless most willing to admit that our Reformers, in acting as they did, were directed by a spirit of sound wisdom. The ecclesiastical arrangements and the devotional formularies of a nation should be adapted to a calm, sober, and healthy state of the religious character, and calculated to educate that character among the people. To authorize anything less would amount to the encouragement of an inferior, morbid, and effeminate tone of religion. But it must be remembered that our Reformers did not strip the discipline of the Church of England so bare of all opportunities for the exercise of a more severe and continuous devotion as we have virtually received it. According to their appointment, she possesses he Wednesday and Friday fasts, her solemn eves and saint-day festivals, and her season of abstinence in Lent, of which the first day's service laments the loss and anticipates the restoration of a more godly discipline. These things have of late years fallen into disuse. They never seem to have revived after the temporary suppression to which they were subjected during the domination of the Puritans. And, besides these holy days and seasons, our Reformers left a wide margin for the operation of individual piety; and that they intended a liberal use to be made of that margin, is evident from the approbation bestowed by the persons who lived nearest to the age, and were more fully animated with the spirit of our Reformation, on the self-denying religion of George Herbert, or on the religious observances of Gidden Hall, within the walls of which the Ferrar family never allowed the voice of prayer and praise to cease, and the Book of Psalms was daily repeated. At the present day such strictness would be condemned as ascetic, and some slighting appellation would be attached to it. The great and wise men who presided over the restoration of our Church were differently affected. They entertained a more tender reverence for the various dispositions and tempers of their brother Christians; and, while they sanctioned nothing less than the most sound and practical reason could approve in our public ordinances, they were willing to allow the most liberal measures of indulgence which the infinite diversity of human character could require, to the exercise of private discipline and devotion. And I hold that your very position as members of the Church of England, binds you to follow their example in this respect. It imposes on all of you, for whom the ordinances of our national religion are sufficient, with whose moral temperament they accord, the duty of exercising an enlarged Christian forbearance towards all those who belong to our communion, but who, either from natural disposition, or from the peculiarity of their education, or from the influence of afflictive circumstances, find the want of something more than is afforded in her existing institutions and customary services. As long as these, your brethren, think the same thing with yourselves—as long as they hold the faith delivered in the creeds, without any sacrifice or truth or introduction of error-you are bound not only to tolerate but to second every effort that they may make towards obtaining for themselves those devotional helps which the Church has not supplied, and providing for those spiritual wants which the Church has not anticipated. The strictly reasonable and the consequently exclusive character of our national form of Christianity demands this charitable indulgence on our part.

This indulgence I would extend to all points of religion which merely relate to devotional discipline, and by which no vital doctrine of the Gospel is either impugned or endangered. Whatever a brother Christian may consider essential to his spiritual welfare, either as a security against the fascinations of the world, or as a course of penitential exercise, or as a means of facilitating his religious progress, we should not only be ready to concede without a cavil or a murmur, but should, if necessary, freely assist him in attaining.... And, at all events, let us not by our censure or our ridicule impose any obstacles in the way of our brother Christians, to prevent them from obtaining those helps to their religious progress which, however insignificant they may appear to us, are of material consequence to them, and which if refused in the English Church, their spiritual home, will certainly be sought elsewhere, either in a foreign communion or by the formation of a new sect.

Now, that extension of kindness, which I would claim for our brother Christians in consideration of the weaknesses of human nature and the diversities of human character, is an indulgence which very many of those who rank among the most orthodox members of the Church of England seem very ill disposed to grant. Our religion, as I have said, addresses itself in a most peculiar manner to the common sense of the people; and there is associated with it, in the breast of many among us, a hard, severe, and uncompromising spirit—a sort of *bigotry of common sense*—which renders them as little lenient as if they were subject to the bigotry of superstition itself. They do not persecute, but they are intolerant. They will make no allowances for those whose devotional feelings, claims, and tastes, do not in every respect coincide with their own. They not only believe themselves to be right, as every bigot does; but, on the supposition that all Christians are men of clear conscience and sound understanding, they are able to prove themselves in the right, which no other bigot can; and they will yield nothing to the weakness of their brethren. Every religious matter is regarded with reference to persons of their own cast of character; and, unless its utility to them can be made apparent, they are very little inclined to take into consideration how far it may or may not be advantageous to others. I do not fear, though with shame, to say that such a spiritual state of mind is very prevalent among our orthodox brethren of the English Church, and it has proved most pernicious to her interests. It is the opponent of all religious feelings which do not evince themselves in accordance with certain conventional rules, and of all religious exertions which are not confined within a certain prescribed and beaten track. It has diminished, and is tending to diminish, the numbers of our fold. In the last century it forced the Wesleyans into schism; it has driven hundreds over to Popery; and, if not relaxed, it will compel a very large body of pious and enlightened Christians to withdraw from our communion, and form a separate Church. I need not say that a spiritual condition thus intolerant and pregnant with mischief is a very dangerous condition. It must be striven against and overcome, not only for the sake of Christian peace and concord upon earth, but for the sake of our eternal welfare in Heaven; for however free such a state may be from the taint of those vices which might dishonor our Christian profession, it is defective in an essential attribute of that grace of charity which is indispensable to the Christian character.

After what I have said, it can hardly be necessary that I should warn you, for the sake of promoting Christian unity, against the practice which is now becoming so general, of attaching yourself to any religious party. You are a member of Christ's body, the Church: —be content with that holy bond of brotherhood. Do not incur the risk of abridging the wide and diffusive spirit of its charity by contracting your sympathies within the limits of any less extended association. To belong to a party in religion is, to say the best of it, and approximation to schism in religion. It appears, indeed, very difficult to understand, how any sincere Christian—who may be well informed respecting the present state of our divisions, and who, before he unite himself with either party, will consider, *first,* whom he is associating himself against—can ever, with a quiet conscience, become a partisan. There are certain principles which distinguish the Churchman from the Dissenter, and which, of course, we hold to be right, or we should not, as honest men, profess to be Churchmen; but could we, on the ground of maintaining those principles, be justified in enrolling ourselves among those who are called the High Church party? Why, among the most prominent members of that party there are individuals who, except that they have not yet acknowledged the Pope's supremacy, or begun to invoke the Virgin, advocate some of the least scriptural doctrines and the most mischievous practices of Romanism. Still less, however, should we do right in arraying ourselves among the opponents of the party, for the great majority consists of men whose views are identical with those of

Cranmer, and Jewel, and Andrews, and Hooker, and Taylor, and Barrow, and all the most eminent names which have served to render the wisdom, the learning, and the piety of our native land illustrious. Or, on the other hand, could we be content to unite ourselves with what is called the Low Church party? Why, among its leaders there are persons holding opinions so directly at variance with the language of the Articles they have signed, of the Liturgy they read, of the rites they minister, and of the Catechism which they are bound to teach, as to render the common discharge of their clerical duties not only incompatible with that grace of spiritual truth which ought to animate a Christian, but of that reverence for moral truth which used to be expected as indispensable to the character of a gentleman. Still less, however, could I endure to associate myself with the undiscriminating opponents of the party; for there are those among them who rank inferior to none in their zeal and activity as disciples of our Savior, whose doctrines are strictly consistent with the teaching of the Church, and whom nothing but a common dread of Popery could have banded in heterogeneous connection with their present Rationalizing and Calvinistic companions. I doubt whether a strictly just and conscientious Christian, if he fairly asked himself the question, "With whom, and against whom, am I combining?" would venture to enroll himself on the lists of any party whatever: I am quite sure he never would with any religious party.

The last brief rule which I should recommend to your adoption, as a means of promoting Christian concord, is to avoid the use of all those vague and undefinable terms which are in such frequent circulation at the present day. "High Church," "Low Church," "Tractarian,"

"Evangelical," "Oxford School," "Protestant Faith," * are phrases which we hear repeated in every society; but what do they mean? Are there any two persons who receive them entirely in the same sense? Is there one man in twenty who connects any distinct ideas at all with the expressions as he utters them? No; but whether understood, or misunderstood, or incapable of being understood, they equally redound to mischief, and, as the watchwords of party, become the fruitful germs of schismatical malevolence. If, therefore, you would do your best to promote the recovery of Christian charity and unity, avoid the use of all such invidious expressions.

But I believe that no steps towards securing that brotherly unanimity among Christians, which our Savior has *enjoined* and *prayed for,* will ever prove effectual without the interference of the authorities. Unless the clergy be compelled to speak the same thing, the laity will never be of one mind. Articles of religion, forms of public worship, catechetical instructions, books of homilies, have been prepared by divines of the most unquestionable learning and judgment for the use of the Church. They contain that scheme of Christian doctrine which was taught in apostolic times by apostolic men,

---

Harness adds the following note: *The use of the expression, *"Protestant Faith,"* is producing great mischief. Christians are learning from it to imagine, that what they *protest against* or *deny* is of more importance to their salvation than what they *believe*; to take credit for the purity of their faith, in proportion as they reject more and accept less than their neighbors; and to consider themselves right in making common cause with those who deny the most vital articles of the creed of the Church, if they are but opposed to those who have added some erroneous articles to it.

which has been approved by the most eminent theologians, which is maintained by an immense majority of Christ's disciples, and which has been found, on careful examination, to be more consistent than any other with the language and the spirit of the *whole* of the Bible. These formularies were composed not only to afford the clergy guidance and assistance in the performance of their duties, but to restrain them from giving way to their own wild fancies, and to secure among them, for the benefit of the people, an uniformity of teaching. The Book of Common Prayer and the Book of Homilies convey the authoritative declaration of the mind of the Church; and a strict adherence to the principles they express ought to be made compulsory on all her ministers. As long as the clergy shall be permitted to deviate, as they please, from the distinctly enunciated doctrines of the Church; we shall hope in vain to witness the blessings of religious concord among their congregations: —and that they should be subject to some control, is demanded by the very circumstances of their position.

Every student of that eminently suggestive book, the Bible, will from time to time conceive that he has discovered some new theory of interpretation, or caught sight of some latent scheme, by which the high mysteries of revelation may be brought more on a level with the capacities of mankind; and if he entertain but little reverence for authority, if he have a strong attachment to his own opinions, and if he be exempt from any check of ecclesiastical discipline, he will not hesitate in disturbing the received principles of his flock by promulgating, as they arise, his fantastic notions from the pulpit. Set the theological imagination loose from all control, and we shall see no end to the extravagant and discordant doctrines which, based on a few slight and disconnected intimations of Scripture, will soon be scattered abroad by the clergy themselves, as the seeds of division among the people.

If the minister possess an active and inventive cast of mind, the evil, in all probability, would be of slight account. His novel inventions would flow in so fast, that the one would rapidly follow upon and drive out the other, and none would have time to take effect. A man of this description carries his own corrective along with him. As his years advance and his understanding steadies, he becomes ashamed of his multitudinous devices. He feels humbled at the recollection of their wildness and their inconsistency. He seeks for instructors of better judgment than his own; and he at length finds rest for his perturbed spirit in the dogmatic teaching of the Church. The danger of conceding too much license to private opinion in religion is not to be apprehended from men of a very lively and ingenious intellect, but from persons of a very inferior mental caliber. The mischief ensues, when a man of limited knowledge and uninventive faculties lights, by some strange accident, on an exploded heresy, and mistakes it for an original idea. It comes upon him like an inspiration; it exalts him in his own esteem as a great discoverer of truth; it is dear to him as an only child; it possesses him like a monomania; and to declare it, is regarded as his particular and Heaven-appointed mission. To characters of this class—narrow-minded and prejudiced, strong in self-conceit, and insensible to argument—many of our diversities of doctrine may be traced; and the peace of the Church demands that their teaching should be subjected to restriction.

But these are sincere and honest dissentients; and they really constitute a very inconsiderable part of the authors of confusion who exist among us. There are others—a large body of men—who are neither sincere nor honest in the dissemination of their heterodox views, and who receive a most pernicious enfranchisement by our present miserable relaxation of doctrinal discipline. An authority is not only required to protect the people against the erring judgment of the clergy, but against their imperfect knowledge, their presumption, their vanity, their love of notoriety, their affectation of novelty, their concession to popular opinion, their false notions of liberality, and their sycophancy to the dispensers of preferment; all these, and many other suggestions of a worldly spirit, will conspire to divert their instruction from that straight line of Church principles which they are bound by their duty to follow, and within the limits of which they ought, for the sake of Gospel truth and Christian peace, to be restrained by some stringent rule of ecclesiastical government.

The English Church never can be clear of the guilt of that *false doctrine, heresy,* and *schism,* which she deprecates in the Litany, or enjoy the *rest* and *quietness* for which she daily prays, as long as impunity is granted to that unbridled liberty of preaching what they choose which has for the last few years been arrogated to themselves by her ministers. While one of that body is allowed to depreciate the apostolic validity of his own orders; another to impugn the spiritual efficacy of the sacraments; another to proclaim his doubts of our Lord's divinity; another, after baptizing an infant at the font, to mount the pulpit and malign the service which he has just been reading; and another to address his congregation in a series of lectures against the Prayer Book (all these irregularities have recently occurred): —whilst such gross *indecencies* as these are permitted to pass, not only unpunished or unrebuked, but even unnoticed—what other consequence can any reasonable man expect, than that the nation should be disturbed by religious dissensions? Under the present circumstances, it is impossible that the people should be of one mind. Divisions on religion are preached, cherished, and virtually inculcated on them as a duty by the clergy. To restore the peace of the Church, the ministers of the Church must be made to render the Articles, the Catechism, the Liturgy, the Homilies, that respect which is due to them, on account not merely of the erudition and the wisdom of the men by whom they were composed, and their perfect agreement with the doctrines of primitive antiquity, but on account of their distinct scriptural authority. Formularies supported by such sanctions, *deserve* our reverence; they will receive reverence from all but the conceited and arrogant; and from them that reverence ought to be enforced by the temporal head of the Church, within whose ability I must believe it lies.*

---

*The king's declaration which prefaces the Articles "requires all his loving subjects to continue in the uniform profession thereof, and prohibiting the least difference from the said Articles"; and also directs that "no man hereafter shall either print, or preach, to draw the Article aside any way, but shall submit to it in the plain and full meaning thereof: and shall not put his own sense or comment to be the meaning of the Article, but shall take it in the literal and grammatical sense." Surely these injunctions might be enforced.

But we are told that there always has been a wider license allowed. Maybe so. But till now the mischief of that wide license has never made itself so bitterly felt; and the experience of the mischief demands the abridgment of the license. Again it is said, "If such severe measures are adopted, will not many honest and pious men be driven out of the ministry?" This might be the case; and it would be an evil, a very serious evil; but by no means so great an evil as their continuing among us and perpetuating our differences. For better would it be for the Church that they should withdraw themselves from her membership and become open enemies, than that they should be allowed to remain within her pale, to create strife among her children, to turn the advantages of their position against her, and to bring her faith and worship into contempt. Besides, if the teaching of our formularies may be departed from, or spoken against with impunity, why do they exist? Why are forms of public worship appointed, but that they should express the sentiments of the men who read and the congregation who hear them? Why is a catechism ever composed, but that it should be taught by those who not only accept the principles which it contains, but desire to extend the knowledge of them? Why are articles of religion framed, but that honest heretics may be excluded from the ministry and dishonest heretics compelled to silence? Assent to the doctrines of the Church is an indispensable qualification for a minister of the Church; and unless that qualification be universally demanded by the temporal power of the Church, the discords of the pulpit never will be suppressed, nor the religious concord of the nation be restored.

This exercise of ecclesiastical authority is required,

not only for the sake of peace and quietness, but for the sake of the spiritual welfare of the people. A religion in discussion never will have force as a practical religion. A disputed creed may engage the minds of the people, but will never reach their hearts: it may afford them matter for conversation, but it will never prove a principle of action. As long as diversities of doctrine exist unchecked, the vital and sanctifying influences of the Gospel will be rendered ineffective. Controversial zeal will continue to be what it has now become, the prevalent religious disposition of the people; and I doubt whether any disposition could be named which is more unfavorable to the great interests of their salvation. Controversy, in all its elements, is essentially opposed to piety. It originates in self-opinion; it extinguishes charity; and it subjects its victims to the most miserable spiritual delusion, by attaching their souls more and more closely to the world, while all their thoughts, words, and actions appear to be engaged with the concerns of religion. Far better would it be for the eternal welfare of the nation, not only of the unlettered, but of the educated classes, that their faith in the Gospel should be held heartily and peacefully, even though intermingled with some error, than that its great and all important truths should be entertained in the manner they now are, as subjects of continual discussion, and of that *uncertainty* which is not only inseparable from such discussion, but by which they are rendered inoperative for good either with regard to this world or the next. The millions of our countrymen are reduced to the state of Pilate; they are taught to doubt *"what truth is,"* by result of such a temper of mind has been predicted by Sir Walter Raleigh. "When," he says, "the truth, which is but one, shall appear to the simple multitude no less variable than contrary to itself; the faith of men will soon after die away by degrees, and all religion be held in scorn and contempt" (History of the World, b. ii, c. 5, s. 1).

Every one of us who is in a situation to form an opinion on the subject, must see that the people are gradually sinking into that appalling state of unbelief which Raleigh has described: "The faith of men is dying away by degrees." And may not our divisions be assigned as the primary cause of the evil? To reduce those divisions, in spite of all regard for family connection, or political party, or exalted station, or any consideration whatever except Christian peace and concord, is the imperative duty of the highest ecclesiastical authority of the nation. There is ample room for skeptical or fanatical speculation afforded by our plenary toleration of the innumerable dissenting sects. Among them all our propounders of unsound doctrine may find their appropriate places; but let them not, for very shame, be permitted to raise their jarring voices within the hallowed precincts of Christ's fold, to disturb the faith and charity of his flock. There could be no hardship in such exclusion. Acceptance of the dogmatical teaching of the Church is one of the qualifications which the Church requires of her ministers; and he who cannot accept her doctrines is as devoid of an essential qualification for the ministry, as if he had wanted eyes to read or a tongue to preach the Gospel.

But as exclusion on such grounds would be no injustice to the clergy, so is it demanded as an act of especial justice to the laity. Are they never to be considered? Is there no duty owing to them? What is the character of the conduct practiced towards the inhabitants of a parish when an incumbent is placed among them, who holds and preaches doctrines contrary to those of the Prayer Book? The lay member of the Church has been himself educated in the principles of the Catechism. He is directed by the Church to teach those principles to his children; and he has a *right* to expect that those principles which he, in compliance with the demands of the Church, endeavors to inculcate as a father, should be further enforced by the consistent instructions of his minister. Has he not, then, ample grounds to complain of injustice; if he find, as is the case with more than one friend of my own, that those religious doctrines which he teaches his family from the Prayer Book at home are almost every Sunday, in some form or other, contradicted in the sermons of his parish priest from the pulpit? This is not the way by which Christian peace and unity ever can be advanced; and I repeat, that till the heterodoxy of the clergy be silenced by authority, there is little hope of our enjoying the blessing of Christian unity.

But though such, to our human view, would appear the probable course of events, we know that nothing is impossible to God; that the hearts, and minds, and consciences of his creatures are subject to his rule and governance; and that the rule and governance of his superintending providence may be influenced by the humble and earnest supplications of those who love and fear him. Under the impression, then, of these convictions, let us place our trust in him; and, exerting every effort in our power to check the contagion of religious discord, and to promote the diffusion of religious peace, let us join in the spirit of the words of our blessed Lord, and pray that all who believe in him may be one, "even as he and the

Father are one" (John 17:11, 21).

CHAPTER 4
THE UNITY OF THE CHURCH
by Baptist Wriothesley Noel
(One Example of an Argument in support of
the "Invisible" Church—This Approach Highly Recommended!)

God has laid down very plainly, the following passages of his word, the marks by which his children may be known from all others. *If we confess our sins, he is faithful and just to forgive us our sins, and to cleanse us from all unrighteousness. If we say that we have not sinned, we make him a liar, and his word is not in us (1 John 1:9-10). He that believeth on the Son hath everlasting life: and he that believeth not the Son shall not see life; but the wrath of God abideth on him. Ye are all the children of God, by faith in Christ Jesus (John 3:36). Whosoever, therefore, shall confess me before men, him will I confess also before my Father which is in heaven. But whosoever shall deny me before men, him will I also deny before my Father which is in heaven (Matt. 10:32-33). They that are after the flesh cannot please God. But ye are not in the flesh, but in the Spirit, if so be that the Spirit of God dwell in you. Now if any man have not the Spirit of Christ, he is none of his. For as many as are led by the Spirit of God, they are the sons of God (Rom. 8:8-9, 14). Hereby we know that he abideth in us by the Spirit, which he hath given us. Hereby know we that we dwell in him, and he in us, because he hath given us of this Spirit (1 John 3:24; 4:13). Now the works of the flesh are manifest, which are these; adultery, fornication, uncleanness, lasciviousness, idolatry, witchcraft, hatred, variance, emulations, wrath, strife, seditions, heresies, envying, murders, drunkenness, revellings, and such life; of the which I tell you, as I have also told you in time past, that they which do such things shall not inherit the kingdom of God. But the fruit of the Spirit is love, joy, peace, longsuffering, gentleness, goodness, faith, meekness, temperance.... And they that are Christ's have crucified the flesh, with the affections and lusts (Gal. 5:19-24). Then said Jesus to his disciples, if any man will come after me, let him deny himself and take up his cross and follow me (Matt. 16:24). Love not the world, neither the things that are in the world. If any man love the world, the love of the Father is not in him (1 John 2:15). Know ye not that the friendship of the world is enmity with God? Whosoever, therefore, will be a friend of the world, is the enemy of God (James 4:4). If ye forgive men their trespasses, your heavenly Father will also forgive you, but if ye forgive not men their trespasses, neither will your Father forgive your trespasses (Matt. 6:14-15). God is love, and he that dwelleth in love, dwelleth in God, and God in him. We love him, because he first loved us (1 John 4:16, 19). He that saith he is in the light and hateth his brother, is in darkness even until now. He that loveth his brother, abideth in the light (1*

John 2:9-10). We know that we have passed from death unto life, because we love the brethren. He that loveth not his brother abideth in death (1 John 3:14). Hereby we do know that we know him, if we keep his commandments. He that saith I know him, and keepeth not his commandments, is a liar, and the truth is not in him. Whosoever abideth in him sinneth not: whosoever sinneth hat not seen him, neither known him (1 John 2:3-4, 3:6). Those, therefore, in whom these scriptural marks of regeneration appear are the children of God, and the disciples of Christ; and those in whom they do not appear are the enemies of God and of Christ. If any man is proud, and self-righteous, or denies the doctrines of grace, or proves that he has not the Spirit of God, by his irreligious tempers and habits, or indulges his passions, and does not exercise Christian self-denial, or is of a worldly spirit, or does not love the children of God, he is no child of God. If, on the contrary, any man confesses his sins, relies exclusively on Christ for his salvation, if he maintains the doctrines of grace and upholds the authority of Christ in the world; if he proves by Christian tempers and habits, that he is governed by the Spirit of God, if he loves all good men, and habitually obeys the law of God, he is a Christian.

All such persons, by whatever other peculiarities they may be marked, are the children of God. *Every one that doeth righteousness is born of him (1 John 2:29). Ye are all the children of God by faith in Christ Jesus (Gal. 3:26). As many as are led by the Spirit of God they are the sons of God (Rom. 8:14).* All such persons are disciples of Christ. *All mine are thine, and thine are mine (John 27:10).* They are all the body of which Christ is the head. *For by one Spirit are we all baptized into one body (1 Cor. 12:13).* And this one body is the church. *He hath put all things under his feet, and gave him to be the head over all things to the church which is his body (Eph. 1:22-23).* Christ, therefore, hath loved them all, and given himself for them all: he has prepared for each of them a place in heaven, and will eventually receive them to himself (Eph. 5:25-27; John 14:1-3; 1 Pet. 1:4-5). No others in the world love or serve him as they do. No others are animated by his Spirit or live to his Glory. Can we be children of God if we do not love them? *Every one that loveth him that begat loveth him also that is begotten of him; by this we know that we love the children of God, when we love God (1 John 5:1-2).* Can we be disciples of Christ, if we do not love them? *By this shall all men know that ye are my disciples, if ye have love one to another (John 13:35).*

We are bound then to love all who bear this character. We are to feel for them as one member of the body feels for another. If one member suffer, all the members should suffer with it; or one member be honored, all the members should rejoice with it (1 Cor. 12). We should all speak the same thing; there should be no divisions among us. We should be perfectly joined together in the same mind and in the same judgment (1 Cor. 1:10). To have envying, strife, and division with them, is to be carnal, and to live as unregenerate persons (1 Cor. 3:3). In our intercourse with them we are *to keep the unity of the Spirit in the bond of peace (Eph. 4:3).* It is the prayer and will of Christ that we should be ONE. *Neither pray I for these alone, but for them also which shall believe on me through their word; that they all may be one; as thou, Father, art in me and I in thee, that they also may be one in us: that the world may believe that thou hast sent me. And the glory which thou gavest me I have given them; that they may be one, even as we are one: I in them and thou in me, that they may be made perfect in one, and that the world may know that thou hast sent me, and hast loved them as thou has loved me (John 17:20-23).*

  The least which all these directions of Scripture imply is, that however separated and distinguished from us such persons may be, by interests, habits, or opinions, by rank, or wealth, or nation, we should own them before the world as our brethren, bear with their infirmities, sympathize with their sorrows, support and help them, vindicate their reputation from unjust imputations, honor them, and promote their happiness, choose their society, and rejoice in their welfare. They imply that being united with them in the great doctrines of the Gospel, we should also be united with them in heart, in brotherly intercourse, and in Christian effort. The prayer of our blessed Savior means far more than all this, but all this is obviously included in it.

  Believers are not ONE, if they are divided in heart, in profession, or in action. If they cannot act together, openly acknowledge each other to be brethren, and live in mutual esteem, they are not ONE. Ungodly persons, with all that is anti-social and repulsive in the prevailing selfishness of our fallen nature, may be more united than they are: and if we are thus separated from those who bear the Christian character, we have great reason to question whether we are ourselves Christians. May, our Lord has assured us, may be thought by others, and may think themselves Christians, who are not so (Matt. 7:22-23; 22:11-13; 25:44-45; Rev. 3:1, 17). Nature may closely imitate grace; and we have great reason to suspect that we still only have a name to live while we are dead, if we hate instead of loving, or are even indifferent and unjust to those who are dear to Christ, and will share in his glory. Vain is all unsanctified learning, vain all spurious zeal, vain all sectarian activity, without love for Christian character. *Though I speak with the tongues of men and of angels, and have not charity, I am become as sounding brass or a tinkling cymbal. And though I have the gift of prophecy, and understand all mysteries and all knowledge; and though I have all faith, so that I could remove mountains, and have not charity, I am nothing. And though I bestow all my goods to feed the poor, and though I give my body to be burned, and have not charity, it profiteth me nothing (1 Cor. 13:1-3).*

Can this be even questioned by any who are taught of God? *As touching brotherly love ye need not that I write unto you: for ye yourselves are taught of God to love one another (1 Thess. 4:9).* This teaching precludes all argument. Those who have much of the Spirit of Christ love each other with an affection which has no parallel in the world. They do not ask why they should love; they cannot help loving. They do not strive to surmount the obstacles to mutual kindness; those obstacles have vanished. They have on Lord, one faith, one baptism, one God, one Spirit, one hope; and what are all their differences?

But if it be freely admitted that we should be united in heart and action with all consistent Christians, do we owe the same brotherly kindness and frank co-operation to those who fall into error? I answer, that there are some errors which imply a hatred of the Gospel, which involve a perversion of the plain statements of revelation, and which are plainly inconsistent with Christian dispositions. To such unbelief, which is a moral offence against God of the worst character, our Lord has attached the most awful penalty. *He that believeth not shall be damned (Mark 16:16).* But there are others, arising from the obscurity of the subject, and from the infirmities of our understandings, which are not inconsistent with the love of the Gospel, which do not hinder the exercise of every Christian grace, and which are found in ALL the children of God. Who can venture to say he is free from error? And if not, how can he condemn another for what he does not blame in himself? From those who fall into the former errors we are commanded to separate. *If any man come unto you, and bring not this doctrine, receive him not into your house, neither bid him God speed (2 John 10).* Those who fall into the latter, we are forbidden to judge, and are commanded to cherish. *One believeth that he may eat all things; another, who is weak, eateth herbs. Let not him that eateth, despise him that eateth not; and let not him which eateth not, judge him that eateth: for God has received him. Who are thou that judgest another man's servant? To his own master he standeth or falleth. Wherefore receive ye one another, as Christ also received us, to the glory of God (Rom. 14:2-4; 15:7).* To judge of the character of an error, we should ask ourselves whether the evidence on the subject is abundant and plain; whether the error implies a disbelief of other great doctrines of the Gospel; whether it is inconsistent with a love for divine truth; whether the person holding it is destitute of the scriptural marks of piety; whether all other good men have been agreed against it; and, finally, whether we are quite sure that it is an error? If, after these inquires, we find that the person whom we suppose to be in error has the clear scripture marks of regeneration, then instead of separating from him, we are obliged, if we would not resist the command of God to *receive him as Christ has received us.* For wherein has he offended? A man, for instance, who bears in his character and conduct all the scriptural marks of a child of God, has been anxious to discover whether it was the will of God that he should baptize his child in infancy. After searching the Scriptures, after reading what has been written on both sides, after conversing with instructed men, and after much prayer, he comes to the conviction, that, according to Christ's institution, his children should be baptized upon their own profession of faith as soon as it is apparent that they believe in Christ, and not upon their parent's profession in their infancy; and he determines that he will not baptize his infant child. Is this a reason why I should separate from him? What else could he do? He was bound to judge by Scripture. He examined it as carefully and as candidly as I could. He prayed for guidance. He listened to the arguments of Christian men on both sides. The majority of the church of Christ, from the earliest times, had, it is true, sanctioned infant baptism, but excellent and able men had reject it. Many is this country, and a far larger number elsewhere, agreed in that view. To him they appeared to have reason and Scripture on their side. After the most careful examination of the question, it seemed to him the will of Christ that his children should be baptized upon their own profession rather than on his. He wished to obey Christ, to be instructed by the Bible, and to honor the Christian ordinance; and *for these reasons* he delayed the baptism. With his views he was obliged to act so. Whatsoever is not of faith is sin; and to baptize his child, not believing it to be Christ's ordinance, would thus far have been wrong. If there was any sin, it was not in following his opinion, but in forming it. But how did he sin in its formation? What could he do more than read, converse, meditate, and pray with a mind wishing to discover the truth? And all that he did. He did not, therefore, sin; and if I am to separate from him because he rejected infant baptism, I am to separate from a child of God for being faithful to his conscience, to the Bible, and to Christ, and for doing that which he could not help doing without sin.

Another Christian, bearing in his life and character all the marks of a child of God, wished to determine whether he should join the Episcopalian section of the church of Christ, or the Presbyterian. He, too, examined Scripture, weighed the evidence on both sides, conversed with upright and intelligent men in both communions, and prayed to be directed right. After much deliberation, he became convinced that Diocesan Episcopacy has no sanction in the word of God, and that the orders and discipline of the Presbyterian body are most conformed to the usages of the church in the New Testament; that Presbyterian orders are of divine appointment, and that it was the will of Christ that he should be so ordained. With that opinion he became a Presbyterian minister. Am I now to separate from his society? How has he sinned? He was obliged to follow what seemed to him the will of Christ. His conclusions were supported by the decisions of several of the Protestant churches. The Lutheran, Swiss, French, Dutch, and Scotch churches, the church of the Vaudois, and a large and pious section of the American church were all on his side. While, in favor of Episcopacy, besides the church of Rome... and the eastern churches... he found only the church of

England and three or four small sections of the church of Christ elsewhere, who had retained Diocesan Episcopacy. Under these circumstances am I to separate from him? Not to have examined the scripture doctrine would have been sin. Not to have followed the convictions of duty, to which the examination led him, would have been sin. In fidelity to Christ, he was obliged to act as he did; and if I separate from him, I do it only because he did his duty.

And these are two of the most important points which separate Christians. Should they separate them? As well might the brothers of a family be separated by the most trifling difference on some question of taste or literature, while both have honorable, pure, intelligent, and cultivated minds. God forbid that Christians should be so separated any longer. Episcopalians and Presbyterians, Baptists and those who baptize infants, with all others who differ on obscure and undecided points, ought, if they have one Lord, one faith, one baptism, one God, and one hope, under the influence of one Spirit, who sanctifies them all, to be one in profession, in action, and in heart. Contemptuous epithets may be heaped upon this union of good men, but it was the object of Christ's prayer. Specious arguments may be forged against it, but it is plainly enjoined by the word of God. But, how, it may be asked, will you thus maintain the truth or secure the unity of the church? Dissent being an evil, and Episcopacy the most scriptural form of church government, this union of good men of all sects will sanction dissent and undermine Episcopacy. Can that be right? *By this shall all men know that ye are my disciples, if ye have love one to another—that they all may be one, as thou, Father, art in me, and I in thee, that they also may be one in us, that the world may believe that thou hast sent me.* That is answer enough. But, in fact, the establishment of minor truths and the unanimity of sentiment in the church of Christ, instead of being hindered by a previous cordiality between the different sections of the church, mainly depend upon it. The objector wants to see unity in the church; and therefore he would hold no brotherly communion with those who, after examination of the Scriptures, with prayer and reflection, believe that it is the will of the great Head of the church, that they should, on various particulars, dissent from us, allowing us, at the same time, the liberty which they claim for themselves of determining our views of duty solely from the word of God. Their present conduct is determined by a religious regard to the will of God, and can only be altered by showing them from Scripture, that it is not agreeable to his will. They as much believe us to be in error, as they think themselves to be right. To deny them to be members of the body of Christ, to be alienated from them, and to treat them with coldness or with jealousy, while they bear on their character and conduct all the great scriptural marks which prove them to be the children of God, is to do them wrong, to sin against the plain directions of Scripture, and to manifest a spiritual blindness, a want of power to discern Christian character, affording a fearful sign that we have never been taught of God ourselves. Will this recommend our opinions to them? If our spirit is so bad, or our judgment so perverse in this particular, it is the less probable that we have found the truth, in thos points on which we differ from them. Our blindness respecting this one plain duty of brotherly kindness to all who believe in Christ, affords a strong presumption of our liability to mistake on subjects more obscure. This opposes one obstacle to their reception of our views. Then the weak among them cannot fail to be irritated by our injustice, and irritation is very unfavorable to an impartial examination of our arguments. By this mode, all union in the church of Christ seems forever hopeless.

Differences of opinion must arise among thoughtful men, when the evidence on both sides is so partial and obscure. Let them be candid, tolerant, and brotherly to each other. Let them allow each other the right of judging for themselves by the word of God. Let them respect each other's honest opinions thus formed, and then they may be ultimately agreed on minor truths; because united in the belief of the great clear truths of the gospel, and loving each other, each of them will examine with impartiality the evidence for every opinion contrary to his own. Now, on the contrary, alienated from each other, they strive to magnify the points on which they differ, exaggerate on both sides the evils which flow from the views opposite to their own, and controversy becomes bitter and interminable. An intolerant, imperious, and unbrotherly course, which, utterly contrary as it is to the spirit of the gospel, is yet dignified with the name of Churchmanship, is of all things the most calculated to exasperate dissension and to perpetuate error. From this a sectarian, jealous, and uncandid temper grows up on all sides. Arguments and declamation abound, not for *the Church of God, which he hath purchased with his own blood,* but for "our church;" not for *Sion, the city of the living God,* but for "our Sion;" not for the diffusion of the saving name of Christ to the ends of the earth, but for "the dissenting cause," or for "our venerable establishment," that is, since the church consists of its members, our venerable selves. All that is great is forgotten for all that is little, and grand truths that should unite Christians together, lie buried under a mass of exaggerated and unfair imputations, which keep them asunder. *Truth is fallen in the street, and equity cannot enter.*

Let me entreat you, my Christian reader, to do your utmost to arrest this growing evil. Of all spectacles which the world exhibits, not one would be more sublime and lovely than the church of Christ, if it were what he intended it to be. Rescued at an incalculable cost from inconceivable ruin, by Divine love, Christians are meant to represent, in the midst of the prevailing selfishness of the world, the love of Christ. *By this shall all men know that ye are my disciples if ye have love to one another.* Millions of persons, with every conceivable variety of opinions, tempers, habits, and interests, attached to every class of society, filling all sorts of situations, speaking different languages, and inhabiting widely separated countries, all united in brotherly love, living to promote the glory of God, in doing the greatest possible good to each other and to the world—that is what the church should be. Now what is it?

Professed Christians are denying each other's right to the Christian name—laboring to extort, from the most scanty, or rather the most unfavorable evidence, proof that Christians are no Christians. They are contending about money. They are attributing to each other the basest motives where the motives are not apparent. They are widening those differences which have already, for gloomy and disgraceful centuries, made an impassable gulf between them. They come into close conjunction with the enemies of the Gospel to carry on hostilities against its friends. They publish to the world each other's faults: they exaggerate them. They accuse each other of invention and of falsehood. They term each other sectarians, rivals, and enemies. They speak, write, preach against each other. And those who are peaceable look on at the unholy strive, and do nothing. Christian reader, if you feel the love of Christ, if you respect the command of God, if you wish for the welfare of the church, if you desire not to be partakers of other men's sins, if you would regret that the progress of religion should be arrested in the world, set yourself, I entreat you, with all your influence of station, and with all your energies of mind, against this discreditable warfare. Separate from violent men of every party; and unite yourself cordially and openly with all who manifest the mind which was in Christ. Long ago has this course been enjoined. *I beseech you, brethren, mark them which cause divisions and offences, contrary to the doctrine which ye have learned, and avoid them. One is your master, even Christ, and all ye are brethren. Love as brethren. Seeing you have purified your souls in obeying the truth, through the Spirit, unto unfeigned love of the brethren, see that ye love one another with a pure heart, fervently (Rom. 16:17; Matt 23:8; I Pet. 3:8; 1:22).*

What, then, must we do? Must we forego the defense of truths because they are controverted? Must we surrender infant baptism, episcopacy, the principle of an establishment, and all other points which a dissenter may happen to deny? I advocate no such concealment of the truth. But if we wish to maintain the peace of the church of Christ without compromise, let us act upon the following rules: —

    1. Let us maintain the sole authority of Scripture in

all matters of religious truth and duty, otherwise there can be no end of discussions. The moment we substitute any other authority than God himself for the doctrines we hold, or the religious duties to which we are obliged, we come under our Lord's censure, *In vain do they worship me, teaching for doctrines the commandments of men;* we are in imminent danger of *making the commandments of God void by our traditions;* and there is no fixed standard to which we can appeal. God's word is the sole standard of revealed truth, and the entire rule of Christian duty, and woe be to those who either add to it or take from it (Rev. 22:18-19).

2. The right of private judgment necessarily follows from the supremacy of God's word. For, as there is no authorized infallible interpreter, to follow any fallible authorities would be to dishonor the word of God by making them supreme. Being fallible, their judgment may therefore, in some points, oppose the doctrine of Scripture; and if in those points we take their views instead of the Scripture for our guide, we should oppose it too. Thus, with us, the Scripture would cease to be supreme, because, instead of ascertaining its doctrine for ourselves, we should yield to an upstart authority which contradicts it. God has given to no man, and to no set of men, this right of supreme decision, so derogatory to the Bible. Each of us will be judged by that alone. And should we have lived in the denial of any of its truths, or the disregard of any of its precepts, it will be no justification that we followed venerable names. The Word of God ought to have been more venerable than they: why did we disregard it? Scripture is our only ultimate authority for faith and practice. *Let every man be fully persuaded in his own mind, for whatsoever is not*

of faith is sin (Rom. 14:5, 23).

3. Let us bear in mind that God has, in his word, told us plainly who are his children and who are not. To deny, against the evidence of Scripture, those to be his children who really are so, is to be guilty of the sin of schism. If a dissenter bears all the foregoing marks of a child of God, and I, overlooking them all, pronounce him to be no member of Christ, because he is no Episcopalian, I am, in the sight of God, a schismatic; I introduce an unscriptural test of Christian character, and am responsible for all the divisions and heart-burnings in the church of God which must follow from my bigotry. As Christians, they have a right to my esteem and brotherly love: they may demand that I honor them, aid them, vindicate them from unjust aspersions, and do all the kind offices which naturally flow from brotherly love. They are dear to the great Head of the Church, and if, instead of all the esteem and love which is their due, I treat them with unkindness, He who once said to an impetuous enemy of the Gospel, "Saul, Saul, why persecutes thou me?" will not fail to notice a similar bigotry in one who has less excuse for it.

4. Let us not condemn our brethren for a faithful obedience to what they believe to be the will of Christ, as revealed in Scripture.

If we see in others the marks of grace, we ought, in the absence of proof to the contrary, to believe that, in forming their opinions, they have examined Scripture with as much of care and candor, of humility and love of the truth, as we have ourselves, and consequently are no more criminal for their errors than we are for ours; perhaps not so much. And since whatsoever is not of faith is sin, they are bound to act according to their conviction of the meaning of Scripture, and instead of blaming them for differing from us, we ought to honor their fidelity. When the missionary Judson, after much examination and prayer, came to the conclusion that infant baptism is contrary to the will of Christ; and therefore, to be faithful to Christ, hazarded the displeasure of all his dearest friends, renounced the salary which was his only means of support, and threw himself on the care of God, by joining the Baptist body, he was surely entitled to the admiration and love of his Christian brethren, and instead of being cut off from the church on that account as a heretic, he ought to have been more esteemed as faithful, and beloved.

5. We should never impute to our Christian brethren inferences which they disown. Sometimes a mischievous doctrine may arise necessarily out of an error into which a Christian has fallen, and yet, by a happy inconsistency, while he maintains the error, he may deny the inference. We should contend against the error, by showing what mischievous inferences may fairly be drawn from it, but we must not conclude, because we see the connection between the inference and the parent error, that he does. The infirmity may also be on our side, the inference which we think to be real may be only apparent. In this case we should still more seriously offend in imputing them to him. A dissenter, for instance, of devoted piety, may entertain decided objections against the principle of an Establishment. To impute to him, on that account, a hatred of the Church of England, especially if he disclaims it, may be most unjust. He may wish to see the Episcopal Church flourishing in piety and numbers, and may yet hate its connection with the State, because he believes the church to be vitiated, and religion

dishonored by that connection.

6. We should never impute to our Christian brethren corrupt motives, when they are not apparent. A pious dissenter wishes to see the connection between the Church and State dissolved. What right have we to say, that this wish arises from envy or from cupidity? He is in other respects a consistent Christian. It is, therefore, much more likely that he wishes to destroy that connection, because he believes it to interfere with the progress of religion, and to lead to jealousies among the different bodies of professed Christians. Under such circumstances, to impute to him the baser and less probable motive, is uncharitable and unchristian.

7. Let us judge no one hastily.

A period of discussion is usually a period of false witnessing. Controversy excites the passions, and passion invents, exaggerates, and scatters far and wide calumnious imputations: but God has said, *Thou shalt not bear false witness against thy neighbor;* and he who propagates a calumny without investigation, as truly bears false witness as he who invented it. Of a good man it is therefore said, he *backbiteth not with his tongue, nor taketh up a reproach against his neighbor (Psalm 15).* Before we condemn our brother, let us ask full proof that he has done wrong. Before we publish his fault, let us be assured that is the will of God that we should publish it. *Judge not, that ye be not judged. Charity thinketh no evil. Charity rejoiceth not in another's iniquity. Charity covereth a multitude of our brother's sins (Matt. 7:1. 1 Cor. 13. 1 Pet. 4:8).*

8. We should seek friendly intercourse with the best men of every name. Nothing more tends to exasperate our prejudices, to narrow our minds, and make us

deformed and dwarfish creatures, in whom nothing great is to be found, except a swollen and inflamed bigotry, than to read only books of one side, see only men of one party, and collect facts of one complexion. Let us seek the friendship of wise and good men wherever we can find them: let piety alone be a sufficient passport to our hearts. And when we find more worth, wisdom, and devotedness than we possess ourselves, in persons of various parties, in high-churchmen, low-churchmen, and dissenters, differing from each other and from us, in many of their opinions, we necessarily become humble and tolerant; and can love them as we ought, though they may in some things widely differ from us.

9. Let us reflect more frequently on the good which we see in our brethren, than in any of their faults.

10. Let us reprove the faults which we discover in them with tenderness, meekness, and a sincere wish to see them grow in grace, and enjoy the blessing of God.

11. Let us act with them in doing good, as far s we can, without any compromise of principle.

Bear in mind that when our Lord prayed that his people might be one, that unity implied co-operation as well as kindly feelings, because it was a unity so public as to draw the world to believe in him: and as our intellectual infirmities alone, to mention no other causes, ensure a discrepancy of opinion to a certain extent on points which it has pleased God to leave involved in obscurity, therefore it was our Lord's wish that we should be one in heart and action, because one in all fundamental points of faith, notwithstanding that discrepancy.

Let us act with all our brethren in doing what all acknowledge to be right. To circulate the Bible, for instance, at home and abroad, is a work so entirely right, that few pious persons could object to it. To refuse then to associate with our brethren in the discharge of that duty, not because the work itself is wrong, but because men of various denominations combine in it, seems to be a violation of Christian unity. It is not endeavoring to keep the unity of the spirit in the bond of peace, it is refusing to testify the brotherly love by which we ought to be known as Christ's disciples, it is essentially schismatical.

But we may do more than this. It tends still more directly to united Christians, if they associate in the diffusion of acknowledged truths. Real Christians hold many doctrines in common. Let the world see, by their uniting to proclaim them, that they do so far agree. The Religious Tract Society illustrates this. There men, of various denominations, all maintaining various great truths of the Gospel, have, in perfect harmony, for many years, labored to diffuse the knowledge of those truths in which they are agreed; and they deserve well of the church of God for their labors. On the points controverted between them they say nothing. On the forms of church government, and on infant baptism, for instance, they are silent; nor are they called to mention them. They have an object as distinct and definite, as have the founders of an hospital, or of a provident society. Their known object is not to teach all the truths of the New Testament, for the world well knows that they differ on various points, but to teach those great truths on which they are agreed. Each, separately may, by other channels, maintain his separate views on controverted points. He conceals no sentiment; he compromises no truth. But the maintenance of his denominational opinions is not his business there. In this way we may promote Christian unity. By the joint diffusion of all the truths on which we are agreed with our brethren, and by the separate promulgation, in a spirit of moderation and love, of those on which we differ from them; by which, while no truths are kept from the world, it may yet see in how much Christians are agreed.

12. Lastly, let us pray for all our brethren, for their prosperity, temporal and spiritual, for themselves, their families, their churches, and their missions. Their grace will be our gain. The more every part of the church of Christ manifests his spirit, the more truth will triumph; the more Christians will be united; controversy will lose its bitterness, and error its artificial supports. Rejoice then, my Christian reader, with all your heart, in the grace of God, wherever you may witness it, and pray that the Holy Spirit may speedily render the whole church of God resplendent in every land with wisdom, holiness, and love; which may God, of his infinite mercy, grant, through our Lord and Savior Jesus Christ.

CHAPTER 5.

A CALL TO LIVE WITH INTEGRITY
WITHIN THE DISCIPLINE OF ONE'S PARTICULAR MANIFESTATION OF THE VISIBLE CHURCH WHILE AT THE SAME TIME RECOGNIZING, AFFIRMING AND BUILDING THE ONE HOLY UNIVERSAL CHRISTIAN CHURCH

Our Christian Heritage Foundation does not advocate the theology, liturgical practices, doctrines, or polity of any particular "visible church". It does not seek exclusivity but rather to promote the recognition of the inclusivity of the "invisible church", the one holy universal Christian church.

There are no particular sacraments or ordinances advocated by Our Christian Heritage Foundation. On the contrary, each congregant is expected to fulfill such holy ordinances and/or to seek such holy sacraments as the Holy Spirit directs him or her so to do, in such church fellowship and according to such church discipline as the Holy Spirit directs him or her so to do.

Change is to be achieved not through rejection of the old, but rather through finding the eternal within the various manifestations of the old.

The purpose of Our Christian Heritage Foundation is to link through all means of communication a world-wide congregation of Christians of diverse traditions united by God's Holy Spirit, seeking to affirm God's purposes through gaining new awareness of the work of God's Holy Spirit in historical times and in our own.

The more we learn about our Christian heritage, the more we appreciate how much we have in common with Christians of all ages and all time—past, present, and future, and, the more we begin to discern just how superficial our differences may ultimately be. From Paul to Luther, from Augustine to Calvin, from Jerome to Billy Graham, all who are open to the leading of the Holy Spirit in each succeeding generation are prompted by the Spirit to learn, to grow, to progress, and to build upon our Christian heritage in such a way as to contribute toward the fulfillment of God's plan and purpose. And as we as individuals participate and contribute, let us look forward to growing more and more into the likeness of Christ in unity with the Holy Spirit, and let us seek to be a part of, as well as a product of, that plan and purpose.

It is hope that seekers throughout the world will engage in this effort whenever possible, wherever possible, and to the full extent possible, sharing joys, concerns, prayer, mutual encouragement and the fellowship of the Holy Spirit. It is our hope and prayer that the invisible church, the eternal, essential and universal church, existing within the various visible churches might break forth into the consciousness of all Christians. May God's Holy Spirit be poured forth upon many! May that which was in ages past invisible to the larger world, held only in the hearts and minds of God's elect saints and holy martyrs within the many branches of the one holy universal Christian church, may this our Christian heritage now become fully manifest!

—Dr. Byron Perrine, Editor
Our Christian Heritage Foundation

ABOUT THE AUTHOR

The Rev. Dr. Byron Perrine is an ordained minister of the Southern Baptist Church who has served for many years as a bi-vocational pastor and educator. In addition to working as a public school teacher and administrator, Dr. Perrine has served as a teacher and assistant administrator at Oneida Baptist Institute, a private Christian boarding school located in Kentucky. He has preached at various times in Baptist, Lutheran, Presbyterian, and United Methodist Churches, most recently for many years as pastor of the Bird Island United Methodist Church in Bird Island, Minnesota. Dr. Perrine owns and operates the Knights Inn Lodge Resort in Forest City, Iowa, and opens this facility to Christian seminars and workshops. In 2012 he established Our Christian Heritage Foundation which is located at his inn. In addition to publishing activities, Our Christian Heritage Foundation maintains a library of historical bibles, manuscripts, and theological books open to those seeking quiet research time in a peaceful setting at the Foundation's Biblical Studies Center. Dr. Perrine is a devoted husband, father and grandfather.

www.ingramcontent.com/pod-product-compliance
Lightning Source LLC
Chambersburg PA
CBHW071749040426
42446CB00012B/2500